Smyth & Hawk'em

"The seeds of discontent *should never be mixed with the seeds of* datcontent.*"*

—*Yogi Berra*

Also by Connor & Downey

Is Martha Stuart Living?

Martha Stuart's *Better Than You At* Entertaining

re>Wired

Zeguts: Ridiculous Restaurants

Smyth & Hawk'em

A gardening parody

By Tom Connor & Jim Downey

Photographs by J. Barry O'Rourke & Randy O'Rourke

HarperPerennial
A *Division* of HarperCollins*Publishers*

Smyth & Hawk'em

You don't have to garden to enjoy our products. In fact, few if any of the items in our catalog are intended for practical use outdoors, or anywhere else for that matter. Besides, who really has time to spend working in the yard these days? We don't. What we do have time for is making and marketing the finest non-essential accessories for the garden and home—items that lead our customers to exclaim, "This is nonessential. I must have it!" Why? Because gardening

18. *Elder-Care Confinement Arbor*

in America isn't about growing things, it's about buying things. Take, for example, our **Fungus-a-Monthus gift club** or our **Radio-Controlled Indoor Crop Duster.** Should you ever have to venture outside to talk to the gardeners and find yourself far from a bathroom, you'll want to try our **Degrades Fiftysomething Biodegradable Incontinence Pads.** Look also herein for our selection of **Smellingtons,** the classic gardening boots, rendered in two dozen smells and colors. Better yet, come visit our company garden, open to the public 24 hours a day, 365 days a year. It's for sale.

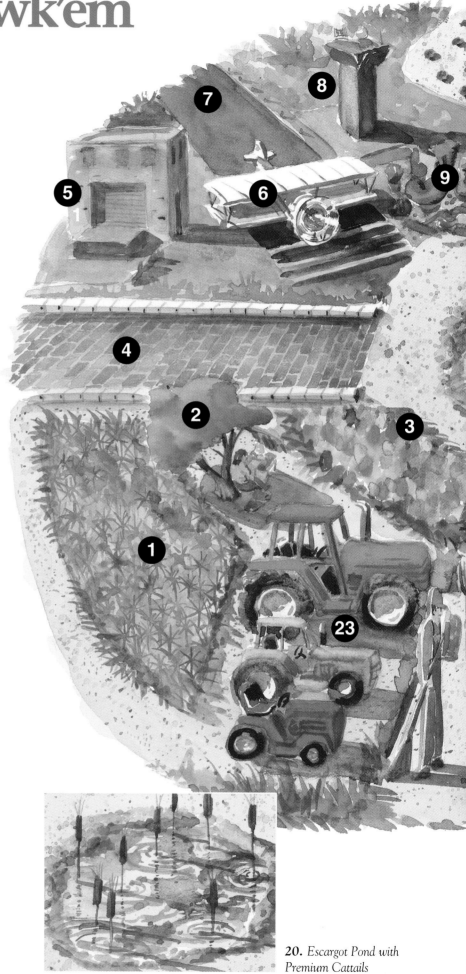

20. *Escargot Pond with Premium Cattails*

1. *Medicinal Marijuana Crop*

12. *Royal Hybrids*

21. *Distressed Bench*

10. *Stepping Scones*

6. *Radio-Controlled Crop Duster*

9. *Sexually Explicit Topiary*

1. Purely Medicinal Marijuana Crop 2. Writing Tree 3. Purely Medicinal Poppies 4. Belgian Block Formal Promenade 5. Shipping & Receiving 6. Radio-Controlled Crop Duster 7. Landing Strip 8. Control Tower 9. Sexually Explicit Topiary 10. Stepping Scones 11. Migrant Workers' Barracks 12. Royal Hybrids 13. Satellite Dish Garden 14. Bio-Grave Composter 15. Casual Promenade 16. Guard Dog Kennel 17. 100 percent Cotton Field 18. Elder-Care Confinement Arbor 19. Bright Plastic Flower Bed 20. Escargot Pond with Premium Cattails 21. Distressed Bench 22. Plywood Gardener Cutouts

Letters from Customers

PROSTHETIC PARTS

Dear Sirs:

This isn't the first time I find myself writing to your company about a product, as you may well recall. That accident with the Smyth & Hawk'em Woodchuck Guillotine Kit last summer has caused me considerable inconvenience, not to mention pain and medical expense. Admittedly, I failed to read the small print about keeping loose clothing and body parts clear of the device. Don't get me wrong, I appreciate the set of replacement blades you sent, though that wasn't exactly what I had in mind. But I must tell you that I do not appreciate seeing in the fall catalog an item I consider personally offensive, given the nature of my loss. Item #P01117, the **Johnson Prosthetic Watering Nozzle,** is a blatant attempt not only to capitalize on my misfortune, but to sell back to me the very unit your company was responsible for my losing. And while the brass fittings and craftsmanship are of superior quality, I'm also offended that it comes only in a three-inch size.

> Yours (as opposed to mine),
> *Scott Johnson*
> *Kennebunkport, Maine*

P.S. "It works pretty well."

JULIA CHIDES

Dear Sirs:

As the greatest chef in the world, my quest for perfectly fresh seasonings has forced me to become a gardener since I refuse to buy the claptrap they sell in stores. As you know, the sooner one gets herbs into the pot after picking, the fresher they taste. So speed is of the essence. Since my garden is almost 400 feet from my house and my physical condition prohibits me from sprinting inside,

I recently purchased the **Smyth & Hawk'em Cast Iron Herb Cannon** so that I could fire herbs straight through my kitchen window from the garden. But I have a question: How do I calibrate the sight on the cannon? The entire side of my house is covered with garlic! This is unacceptable.

> *Julia Child*
> *Cambridge, Mass.*

Dear Julia:
Consider water a beverage instead of your usual Pinot Noir with "big shoulders." Your aim should improve.

VERMONTROGEN

You people:

You people need to spend a little more time in the garden and a little less time going to the bank. Haven't you ever heard of nitrogen?! Cabbages—succulent, lovely orbs that give us the energy of life! Beets—those garnet-colored messengers that bequeath us the energy of life! Broccoli Rabe—that delicious green harbinger of Spring that so willingly gives us the energy of life! These are the things that are important. These are the things that bring us closer to heaven. Not some damn pink Smellingtons! What's wrong with you people? Don't you see what's going on? When I take a bath every year, I put the bath water back in the soil. You think something doesn't *grow* in that spot? When my clothes rot off my body, I plant a seed where they fall. When my teeth fall out of my head, I plant them. Why? NITROGEN!!! When are you people going to get it?

> Wake up and smell the nitrogen!!
> *The guy with the beard from "Victory Garden"*
> *Deere, Vermont*

WHITE HOUSE INVITATION

Dear Sirs:

We are pleased to tender an invite to the good people of Smyth & Hawk'em to come on down to our nation's Capital and be our guests at The White House. We hope that you could take a stroll around the Rose Garden and see what y'all could do to pep it up a bit. We were thinking a little okra might be just the right touch. We would, of course, invite you to sleep in one of the upstairs bedrooms (that's the same floor we sleep on) and you could order room service and keep the towels and make a few calls and tell people what to do and such. It's a really fun night. All we would ask in return from you would be a small contribution, say, $50,000.00.

> *Sincerely,*
> *Bill and Hillary*
> *The White House*

Editor's note: We don't pay, we invoice.

UNHAPPY GARDENER

Dear Señors:

I have a sad tale to tell and I am hoping that you will be able to help me in my plight. I used to work for a very, very famous rich woman in Connecticut. I came to work for her so I could be near the dirt which makes me happy. Soon I was being called out of the garden and sent to the city to pick up cleaning, shampoo the dogs, detail the cars and do many other things I'd rather not mention that I don't think have to do with the garden. She would yell at me very much and tell me if I did not do things the way she wanted, she would have the INS and the IRS and the CIA do bad things to me. So I quit and hired F. Lee Bailey, Johnny

Cochran, and other big guns to help poor Hector collect his back pay. My problem is that I left my shovel, rake and hoe on the woman's property and am afraid to go back. But without them I cannot work. Do you have any old tools I could borrow until I win the $12 million lawsuit? I await your generosity.

Hector Benevides
Out-of-work gardener
Westport, CT

Dear Hector:
Our hearts go out to you in your hour of need. We have taken up a collection among ourselves and are enclosing a brand-new shovel, rake and hoe, along with an invoice for $349 (net 30, please add Connecticut sales tax). This is the cost to us for the equipment. We feel it's the least we can do and still sleep at night. Happy gardening!

SMALL WORLD
Dear Smyth & Hawk'ems:
I am a jockey by trade and prefer to keep my garden in scale with my size. Can you suggest any small versions of astilbe, ajuga, begonia, bleeding heart, blueberry, caladium, clematis, coleus, columbine, coneflower, currant, daylily, dogwood, gloriosa, honeysuckle, hosta, hydrangea, impatiens (especially "African Queen"), ivy, juniper, lettuce, liriope, ferns, pachysandra, torenia, trumpet vine, viburnum, vinca vine and viola? The standard sizes make me feel small.

Freddy Arcaro
Liliput Farms
Watch Hill, Rhode Island

Dear Freddy:
We receive this query a lot, and it's actually moved us to action. Next season, we'll be introducing our first Gardening Stilts, designed with jockeys in mind. They adjust to a height of 6' 1", which, in your case, would bring you face-to-face with a tall sunflower. So if your "corn is as high as an elephant's eye," don't worry. We've got you covered.

DEADHEADED
Hey now:
Since the tragic, cataclysmic and untimely death of Jerry Garcia, I've noticed that my in-bus crop of Cannibis Sativa Ridiculoso seems to have lost its spirit, its *joie de vivre*, its lust for life. I know how it feels because I still haven't snapped out of this ungroovy funk myself. It seems like life's got a little side door that's closed and I can't find the key to it on my chain but I have a lot of keys so I keep trying to open the little door so I can keep on truckin'. In the meantime, what can I do about my hemp, bro? It's feelin down.

Moon Ocean Rock
Bus
Marin County, California

Dear Mr. Rock:
We don't condone the propagation of illegal plants. However, if the plants were in a place where growing them was legal, we would, hypothetically, nip the topmost buds of the largest plants and use them for whatever came to mind. Then we would make a tea of Black Angus manure and honey and spray the remaining plants. This isn't to say this has worked for us in the past, but we think Jerry would approve.

CROCKERY MOCKERY
Dear Sirs:
We have a bone to pick with your company. Why is it that every time we introduce an item, we see it three weeks later in your rag under a different name? We debut our Large Copper Spittoon and it turns up in your book as The Copper Vegetation Orb. What's up with that? And another thing, our reps in Taiwan tell us that your reps are paying manufacturers there not to sell to us. Didn't anybody ever tell you about karma?

The Crockery Barn Catalog
Seattle, Wash.

Editor's Note: It's only business, nothing personal.

HEDGE BET
I was recently acquitted of a serious crime that unfortunately was given national, make that worldwide, attention. I am absolutely 100 percent not guilty, but that doesn't seem to make a damn bit of difference to the ten thousand ***holes that look in my windows every day. Can you suggest a very high hedge, preferably with poisonous properties, with which to keep these *** holes at bay?

Anonymous
Los Angeles

Dear O.J.:
We suggest the large Toxicum Necrosis bush. This malodorous hedge grows like the dickens, smells like overripe limburger, and exudes a mucilagelike substance that rots clothing or anything else it touches. Enclosed please find a starter bush. Unfortunately, we are forced to ship this C.O.D. to you. We trust you will understand.

7

Royal Strain

Four centuries of experimentation and crossbreeding in Her Majesty's greenhouses have produced a number of hybrids that are instantly identifiable and remarkably resistant to change. Over the years, however, the genetic makeup of this venerable family of plants has steadily broken down, leaving each successive generation duller and less appealing, even to bees. They remain, nonetheless, perennial favorites of American gardeners.

The garden

H.R. HIBISCUS

Although cultivated to take over the garden one day, this is perhaps the least successful of the royal hybrids. Bulbs, which are stored in the basement of Windsor Castle until called to service, remain dim much of their lives. Once in bloom, the variety tends to be dwarfed by royal mums and roses, in whose shadows it is usually found. And with its rather large, protuberant side petals and an abnormally small stamen, the male flower frequently has difficulty pollinating female plants.
#R10085 **$30**

QUEEN MUM

Dowdy but regal, this ancient mum continues to reign throughout Great Britain and much of the world, where it is revered as a symbol of a time before the sun set on British gardening. It is distinguishable from other mums by its blue-rinse coloration and mildly perturbing exhalations. Needs staking and periodic repotting.
#R10001 **$190**

ELIZABETHAN ROSE

Also on the dowdy side, and with a reputation for being prickly, this classic English rose nevertheless has a huge following among commoners, who cherish the ground it grows in. Thoroughbred stock and a deep root system ensure that this variety will continue to bloom far longer than other royal plants might hope or wish. Attracts sycophants and small, yippy dogs.
#R10002 **$170**

PRINCESS MUM

Once considered useful only as a container specimen, this beautiful but unstable hybrid has evolved stiff, spinelike outer petals in recent years as a result of proximity to other royal plants, and is now the far more interesting and valuable flower. It requires full sun and near constant attention, however, and can be quite expensive to maintain.

#R10086 **$110**

MR. TOPIARY HEAD

Children frequently demand attention at the very worst times, such as when we're attempting to cultivate inner harmony in the garden. We don't like this. Worse, the negative energy that's generated can do lasting psychic damage to our plants. That's why we developed the Mr. Topiary Head children's garden toy. We'll send you the basic topiary form. While you garden in peace, the kids can create an infinite number of faces out of last night's salad or fun items they find in the compost heap.

Mister Topiary Head Blank *#T35634* **$98**

PRECARVED BEECH TREE

Years after passion cools and young lovers part, marry others, divorce, remarry, grow old, and die, usually alone and embittered, the trunk of the majestic beech tree remembers happier times. Smyth & Hawk'em's copper beeches come fully matured and precarved with your romantic graffiti or ours.

#B84645 **$1,895**

Exotic Flowers

A.

C.

B.

A. LASCIVIA (PRIEST-IN-THE-PULPIT)
Uniform black foliation and asexual characteristics cloak a throbbing red stamen and voracious appetite for trusting, innocent insects. Thrives in full shade and unsupervised sections of the garden.
#E98748 **$53**

B. AMARTHAYLLIS NARCISSUS
Tasteful hues, perfectly shaped foliage, and a carnivorous corolla have brought this plant unparalleled attention and success. Once confined to a tiny region of the Eastern U.S., this narcissus has spread to every growing zone of the planet, overwhelming native plants and other life-forms.
#E56141 **$180**

C. LOBELIA CRUSTACEA
Spiny, salmon-colored projections atop a 20" stalk give off a perfume that reminds some gardeners of shrimp fleets pulling into port. Found only on the northern coast of Maine, often in a bed of snow or ice.
#E66621 **$48**

WRITING TREE

As children, we had a secret place to which we retreated when we wanted to get away from our parents and siblings. It was here that we could do special things, like look at Dad's *National Geographics* or have Ken and Barbie play house. Now that we're grown-ups, we need a private place more than ever. Under the drooping, protective branches of our Writing Tree, you can write letters, solve personal problems, or meet a friend and just do stuff, all far from husbands' and wives' prying eyes.

Writing Tree #T12480 **$840**
Writing Tree Table #T12481 **$120**
Writing Tree Lamp #T12482 **$60**
Writing Tree Carpet #T12483 **$295**
Writing Tree Pen #T12485 **$75**
Writing Tree Ink #T12486 **$12**
Writing Tree Journal #T12487 **$25**
Writing Tree Blouse #T12488 **$40**
Writing Tree Shorts #T12489 **$30**
Writing Tree Panties #12490 **$20**
Writing Tree Cot #T12491 **$170**
Writing Tree Porto-Bidet #T12492 **$225**
Writing Tree Bottled Water Glass #T12484 **$35**

#T12488 & #T12489

#T12485 & #T12487

#T12484

#T12481

#T12482

READING HEDGE

Perhaps you've been inundated with relatives from afar who haven't quite mastered the Queen's English but love to talk anyway. Or maybe your spouse is in one of his or her special moods, requiring a hasty exit on your part until his or her medication kicks in. Either is the perfect time to head out to our Reading Hedge. When planted far enough from the main house and family life, this variety lets in just the right amount of light (roughly the equivalent of F3.8 on a bright, sunny day) for reading Chopra, Freud, or Jung. #H39399 **$640**

CUSTOM SWAMPS

Inland seas, marshes, bogs, and swamps once covered the North American suburbs, making most of the continent one big petri dish of primordial bouillabaisse. Twentieth-century land development and landscaping practices filled in most of the surviving swamps with rocks, garbage, topsoil, grass, and shrubbery, but in the 1990s, property owners began expressing a deep longing for their watery roots. Now, ornamental ponds and artificial streams are gradually declaiming the land. Our custom swamps take advantage of preexisting wetlands under homeowners' lawns to create the ultimate in water gardens. If you have an acre or more of under- or overutilized property, we'll turn it into a soggy, boggy, funky mess teeming with the stuff of environmentalists' dreams.

Acre-Custom Swamp #S00220 *(beginning at)* **$45,995**

Swamp Water #S00221 *(approximately 30,000 gallons)* **$18,725**

Bottled Swamp Water #S00222 **$37,350**

Lily Pads #S00223 *(per bushel)* **$195**

Eel Grass #S00224 *(per peck)* **$120**

Eels #S00225 *(per gross)* **$160**

Family of Carp #S00226 **$20**

Amphibia #S00227 *(set of two of each species)* **$225**

Mosquito Colony #S00228 *(per case of one zillion)* **$25**

Fungus-a-Monthus Gift Subscriptions

Twelve months of glorious cryptogams

Cryptogams are single-cell, nonflowering plants grown from spores and include the large, close families of algae, mosses, fungi, lichen, rust, and pond scum. Cryptic, exotic, and usually asexual, they are perfect gifts for the 90s. They require no earth, water, light, warmth, air, or care. They take nothing and give nothing in return. A gift of fungi is the right gift for someone who habitually kills houseplants, and a wonderful way of telling people like that how you feel—month after month after month. Our twelve-month offering brings a selection of rust in January, blue mold in February, moss in March, spornucopia in April, algae in May, lichen in June, pond scum in July, puff balls in August, smut in September, toadstools in October, tree fungus in November, and scales in December. These wonderful gifts come with Velcro backing for easy mounting. Whether displayed on a coffee table or attached to a tree, wall, or refrigerator door, fungi and their kind will last forever and reproduce at will. *Twelve-month gift selection* **#F64005** **$285**

October

November

November

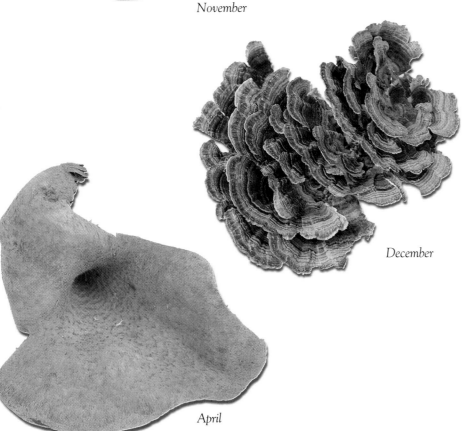

December

April

15

50S' CLASSIC TWO-TONE SHRUBBERY

Your garden features pink flamingos and your driveway a '57 Chevy Bel-Air. Your doorbell chimes "You ain't nothing but a hound dog" and your garden bird bath is a statue of Elvis in a pose from his farewell Vegas concert. All that's missing is this: our classic Two-Tone Shrubbery from the 50s, which will add that perfect touch of kitsch and have your guests exclaiming, "Solid Jackson!"
#T54637 **$845**

BREADFRUIT TREES

We developed this hardy North American hybrid of the classic tropical fruit tree in response to demands from customers who've moved from New York City and can't find good, fresh pumpernickel or rye in the suburbs of Westchester and Fairfield counties. Planted after the last frost, our breadfruit sapling will grow to a height of 14 feet and produce half a dozen different loaf varieties and sizes by late summer. *#T90558* **$248**

OTHER PEOPLE'S GARDENS

Gardens, like lawns, not only look greener from the other side of the fence, they usually are greener. But why lust after other gardens or, worse, spend years slaving to establish your own, when you can simply buy someone else's? Smyth & Hawk'em's international garden relocation crew continually roams the Continent and British Isles looking for legendary gardens for our customers. These gardens are dug up by night (to avoid sun damage to roots), rolled onto trucks, and driven to the nearest port, then shipped across the Atlantic and unrolled onto your property a week later. Now prize-winning gardening can be as easy as writing a check. *Properties and prices available upon request.*

The previous owner of this property (inset), an impressionable man heavily influenced by nineteenth-century watercolors, spent decades developing the lily ponds and perennial beds of his gardens outside Paris (above). Today he's dead, and his gardens are up for grabs.

17

LITTLE DICKENS LIMB SAW

Frank Lustre, Shipping & Handling

Twelve years ago, I passed a hospital stay by reading the tales of Paul Bunyan. The story awakened in me a man I hadn't known

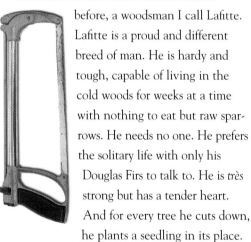

before, a woodsman I call Lafitte. Lafitte is a proud and different breed of man. He is hardy and tough, capable of living in the cold woods for weeks at a time with nothing to eat but raw sparrows. He needs no one. He prefers the solitary life with only his Douglas Firs to talk to. He is *très* strong but has a tender heart. And for every tree he cuts down, he plants a seedling in its place.

When he has felled his daily quotient of trees, he hauls them out to the logging road using only the strength of his back. There he leaves them, caring nothing for compensation, hoping only they will be put to good use to build shelters for orphans. Lafitte's favorite tool? The Little Dickens Limb Saw, which he keeps sharpened to a fare-thee-well. Lately he, I mean I, have been working at slicing extremely thin layers from a large tree trunk. My goal is to slice off a sliver of wood so thin that it will float in the air of its own accord. I'm very close.
#S99978 $36

staff favorites

Over the years, we've noticed that our stock of certain products has dwindled even when there were no orders from customers. Far be it from us to accuse anyone of anything so base as pilferage, but when we asked employees to review the products below, we found that they readily rated their favorites before we had a chance to tell them which ones we wanted reviewed.

MOW DE COLOGNE

Skirmantas Rastas, Animal Husbandry

The beautiful, perfect, wondrous temple that is my body is, after my wife, Felicia, my most prized possession. I bathe it six times daily. In the mornings, I like to add buttermilk to heated springwater for my first two baths (at 8 A.M. and 10 A.M., respectively). For my

two afternoon ablutions, I bathe in a mixture of very cold seawater, ram's blood and grapefruit juice. I find this to be energizing and a great aid to digestion. In the evening, I take a final two baths, the first in heated sawdust, the second in Perrier. Afterwards, I spray my entire body with Mow de Cologne. Felicia says I smell like the Maharaja of Jodhpur, and that is okey-dokey with her.
#C63812 $35

PRESLIMED POTS

Missy Martin, Copy Editor

My absolutely favorite thing is growing petunias in my window garden. When they are in glorious full bloom, all is right with the world. Mother can call, and we won't argue. The butcher may be mean, but his words won't cut me. Cab drivers seem to have happy smiling faces. Even the bums on the street are having a good day. But sometimes, the grey thing happens, and the world gets a coating of what I

can only describe as a smelly, greasy substance that permeates everything. My clothes smell of it, and the sun is black, and food tastes terrible, and I have to go indoors and stay very quiet. The only thing that helps me when the grey thing happens is listening to my Preslimed Flowerpots. When I hear "Whistle while you work" or "When you walk through a storm" coming out of these pots, I feel like I can go on for at least another few hours.
#P47297 $28 *each*

LANDSCAPERS' MOWING PLANK

Alfredo de Riveras, Old Product Development

I grew up in a large family in southern California on the Mexican border. My father worked for a landscaper in Los Angeles, driving one of the pickup trucks that carried the big Locke mowers to job sites in the suburbs. Whenever the wood planks used to off and on-load the mowers grew too weather-beaten or weak to support the Lockes, our family would get them and immediately they would be put back to work around our yard. We fenced the goat and chickens with the planks. We ate meals off rough outdoor tables made out of them. One winter, I remember, we lived in an earthen room in the ground with the planks for our roof. Eventually, my father collected enough mower planks to build a modest, one-story house where we lived until I was 13. To this day, my brothers and sisters and I still pick splinters out of our feet and butts from living in that plank house. After graduating from UCLA with a degree in marketing, I moved north to look for work in the booming home and garden lifestyle industry. Imagine my surprise when I came to Smyth & Hawk'em and found plans under way to market upscale versions of the very planks I spent most of my life surrounded by. Evidently intrigued by my strong reaction to the product, management put me in charge of mower plank development and sales.

#P39930 **$75** *each*

HAPPY LANDINGS BIRDSEED

Robin Grackle, Employee Cafeteria

If I could choose the form of my reincarnation, it would be as a Canada goose or one of the many other winged visitors to the Smyth & Hawk'em company grounds. And, like them, I would never leave on account of this magical birdseed mix we market and sell. As a lifelong aviophile, I have never seen birds so content to be observed, hand-fed, petted, even whacked by children wielding branches or winging stale bread at their heads. So relaxed are they, in fact, that one can literally walk up behind them and lop their heads off with an axe, say, before they're able to pull their little beaks away from this entrancing seed.

One-kilo bag #D76896 **$25**
Refills: **$10** *per hit*

URBAN PRUNING KNIFE

Kim Batten-Hatches, Arborium

As a small boy growing up at the edge of Sherwood Forest, I used to pretend I was Robin by carving declarations of love and other messages for Maid Marian on the massive beech trees then still to be found in those magical woods. I carved these puerile missives with a small penknife my father had purchased for me in London. Later, at St. Onan's School, I used the same knife to carve the names of masters and other students, along with certain messages for them, into the tops of desks and the limbs of younger, frailer boys. When the penknife was confiscated, I was heartbroken. Though I searched all over England, I never was able to find another like it. Until, that is, I came to Smyth & Hawk'em and discovered to my utter delight a knife being offered for sale that was even more wonderful than the knife of my boyhood. I was especially impressed by the option of different typeface blades that can be ordered, particularly the Gothic and Windsor Cursive fonts, and, of course, the standard open-tree surgery blade. But what I most love about our pruning knife is its pure speed. With a simple flick of a button, the blade can be opened almost simultaneously with one's impulse to use it.

#S78981 **$119**

gardening accessories

ELDER-CARE CONFINEMENT ARBOR

Like seasoned perennials that have grown longer in the leaf than in the bulb, many elderly need a firm support system. And with more middle-aged children assuming responsibility for parents and in-laws, there's a growing need for a place for them while boomers garden. Our confinement arbor combines the freedom of the great outdoors with the security of a strict Catholic nursing home. Each unit comes with cuffs and break-out alarm. #E50334 **$160**

"POTTERY-TRAINED" CHILD CONTAINMENT POT

At last, a child-care system that exposes young children to the wonders of nature while permitting Mom and Dad to work in the garden without interruption. High-fired, no-nonsense terracotta is just the thing to thwart even the most active babies. German craftsmanship further renders these pots childproof and virtually inescapable.
Newborn (18 inches high) #L60980 **$48**
Infant (24 inches high) #L60981 **$62**
Toddler (36 inches high) #L60982 **$80**

COPPER VEGETATION ORB

We've been wearing copper wristlets to ward off arthritis, chronic fatigue, Lyme disease, hoof and mouth disease, shingles, Guy de la Roche syndrome, smacker's foot, planter warts, groliosis, and other bodily maladies for years. Now, for the first time, you can apply the curative powers of copper to your mind. This 100 percent hammered-copper orb is the perfect spot to curl up and forget about earthly responsibilities like college tuition, mortgages, car payments, and the like. One hour in the orb has the same therapeutic effect as three sessions of Freudian analysis, five sessions of Jungian dream therapy, or up to twelve sessions with an unlicensed social worker. If used on a daily basis, our orb will pay for itself in just five weeks.
#L44242 **$3,999**

BUNG RAKE CANDLEHOLDER

Many of the tools purchased for our catalogs look great but are never put to practical use. This is because we have no idea what they are or how to use them. Take, for example, this item. What's a bung rake? See? We don't have a clue. But we do know an attractive candleholder when we see one. Made from what we think is tempered steel and possibly hand-forged, the handle end of the tool will accommodate most candle sizes for hours of reading or romantic dining.

Pair of Candleholders #H19180 **$49**

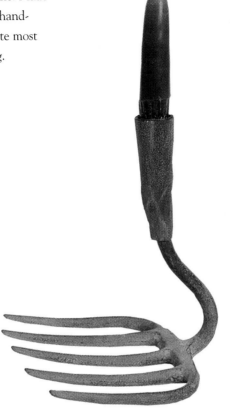

PROFESSIONAL FLOWERING SHRUB & TREE PRESS

This serious, loggers-grade hardwood press will enable you to smash any North or South American species in a matter of seconds. The patented double-screw design exerts enough pressure, in fact, to flatten whole sections of garden, woods, or even small to mid-size vertebrates. Comes with blotters and scrapers. 3 feet wide by 4 feet long.

Shrub & Tree Press #T26015 **$225**
10 Refill Blotters #T26016 **$24**
2 Replacement Scrapers #T26017 **$18**
Selection of Vertebrates (one dozen) #T26018 **$78**

TIME-IS-MONEY CHERUB CLOCK

We can buy houses, gardens, titles, automobiles, lifestyles, even people, but we can't buy time. Time flies and so does money. That's what this charming cherub clock reminds us of day in and day out. Our puckish little messenger carries a highly accurate Swiss-made quartz timepiece between his wings. The clock face can be ordered in dollar signs, yen, deutsche marks, zotlings, dinars, or any currency you cherish.

#C98762 **$345** *(batteries not included)*

BIO-GRAVE COMPOSTER

The ultimate composter, and the last one you'll ever need to purchase. Just add earth, leaves, grass clippings, kitchen scraps, and a corpse, and the Bio-Grave will produce superenriched soil for the garden in just three years. The hinged half-lid permits additional composting and viewing. Bio-Grave measures 6 feet long by 3 feet wide by 3 feet high; holds up to three bodies.

#C11694 **$249**
Three zillion Bio-Grave Maggots #M58772 **$20**

imported gardeners

Gardening is relatively new to this country. More recent still is well-to-do Americans hiring others to garden for them. But for centuries, landowners in Europe and other parts of the world have kept gardening couples on their property, owning or renting them and frequently bequeathing them to their children or passing them along to new owners. Unlike American landscaping crews, these laborers are well groomed and mannered, and are used to long hours, low pay, and little hope of ever transcending their lot in life. Now, for a limited time, we are offering a selection of these superior quality gardening couples for import.

#C11297

#C11296

IRISH GARDENING COUPLE

Jack and Maureen Dunn (*above*) have been gardening together since their youth in Northern Ireland, where their families lived and worked on the grounds of the cruel Lord Nancy, Duke of Worcestershiresauce, a distant cousin to Prince Charles. The Dunns specialize in suggestive topiary but are also trained in creating unusual hybrids. Although a string of bizarre gardening accidents has seemed to follow the couple from estate to estate throughout Great Britain, they are hoping to make a fresh start in the United States. They require only the most basic of shelters and several pints of stout, each, per day.
#C11297   **$43,000**

Also available in:
Latin American Gardening Couple
#C11298   **$54,750**

Japanese Gardening Couple
#C11299   **$107,500**

ENGLISH GARDENING COUPLE

English gardeners Bertie and Reggie Balfour-Waulk, (*left*) are experts in creating and maintaining formal defenestration flower beds. The Balfour-Waulks are available immediately for sale and import.
#C11296   **$97,500**
(add $2,369.98 for shipping)

HAPPY LANDINGS BIRDSEED

We love the look of the lawn when it's covered with a living quilt of avian friends. Too often, however, they fly off the moment their birdseed dinner has been consumed, leaving us wishing we could have more time to observe them in their natural state. We were elated, then, to discover Happy Landings, a seed mix composed of the six most popular and nutritious birdseeds, plus a seventh, more exotic, seed that has a slightly narcotic effect on all winged creatures. After just a couple of beakfuls, they are happy to walk slowly around on the lawn for three to five hours before taking off. And we guarantee they'll quickly get into the habit of coming back for more.

One kilo bag #D76896 **$25**

Additional servings **$10 a hit**

HIGH-VOLTAGE ANTI-SQUIRREL BIRD FEEDER

Go ahead, look out your kitchen window at your bird feeder. See any birdseed in it? We didn't think so. It's not on account of birds having eaten it, but because the local populous of several million squirrels has passed the word that there's a good meal to be had in your backyard. Now, at last, you can win the war against these rats with bushy tails. The moment anything a breadcrumb heavier than eight ounces lands on our feeder, 35,000 unrestricted volts of electricity will course through its verminous little body. After just a few days' use, you'll notice birds happily congregating at the feeder again and a pile of gray cinders around the base. #V65432 **$685**

PLYWOOD GARDENER CUTOUTS

A less expensive alternative to our imported gardeners are these realistic cutouts. The only difference: They're plywood! Yet neighbors and passersby will swear you have real, live gardening help. Cutouts come with stand and movable, battery-powered hands and mouth parts. #C11300 **$230** *each*

RADIO-CONTROLLED INDOOR CROP DUSTER

Does the thought of spraying your half-acre indoor greenhouse for aphids by hand make you want to throw your sprayer through the glass? Take heart, and then take the stick. Now you can dust with your very own gas-powered, radio-controlled, indoor crop duster. This streamlined beauty can lay down a thick layer of anything from Malathion to Agent Orange over a 400 X 400 foot area in a matter of minutes. With a little practice, you'll be the angel of death to any bug that's unlucky enough to wander into your kill zone.

#A45188 **$3,500**

Includes radio control box and videotaped instructions from Chuck Yeager.

AGENT POTPOURRI

Friends tell us this all-purpose agent is best sprayed immediately after planting seedlings, when an ugly hint of manure is likely to hang in the air. Its lovely lavender, patchouli, and old rose scents make waiting for new blossoms, a little more endurable.

#C22267 **$8.50** *per ounce*

PRO-SPEED 750

We've tried everything on the market, but nothing really comes close to Pro-Speed 750 for hastening the growth process in practically any plant. For example, the average elapsed time between planting and bearing fruit for apple tree seedlings sprayed with Pro-Speed is six days, two hours, and 12 minutes.

#C22268 **$33** *per kilo*

BETTY & GEORGE'S SPECIAL APHRO-DAISYACK SPRAY

People always ask what keeps our resident octogenarian couple, Betty and George Howell, looking like a pair of hot, teenage rabbits. The Howells swear their romantic ardor is the result of this homemade spray. Refined from the pistil powder of African Nbwe Usi Jay plants, Aphro-DaisyAck causes hot flashes in anyone who stops long enough to smell the daisies.

#C22269 *One-pound bag* **$55**

MINI-MAX VITAMIN ADDITIVE FOR MINIATURE FOOD CROPS

We love those little ears of corn but hate eating them out of cans. Yet when we've grown our own miniature veggies, we've picked them so early that they had absolutely no nutritional value. This airborne spray we discovered adds vitamins to any diminutive vegetable. It's especially good with miniature rutabaga, broccoli rape, and fiddlehead fern.

#C22270 *Five-pound bag* **$105**

MAGIC MONKEY MANURE MIST

Over the years, we've refined the solid waste of nearly every animal on earth in our quest for the perfect manure. Finally, at long last, we think we've found it! While in Brazil recently to check on our rare-woods logging operation, we noticed a tiny pile of manure with a 12-foot orchid growing from its center. Local natives informed us that this was the dropping of the "Magic Monkey." Now all you have to do is spray it on stubborn plants, then stand back!

#C22272 **$27.75** *per aerial spritz*

Sayr Rampochanyr, chief clansman of the Slovobodrogian pot-slimers.

PRESLIMED POTS

Unlike flowerpots found in old estate greenhouses, which can take decades to properly moss and mold up, our pots are painstakingly hand-slimed by a community of exiled Slovobodrogians living under an unfinished section of the West Side Highway in New York City, then left overnight in the men's room of Grand Central Station before shipping. A favorite of nouveau suburban gardeners, each pot in the series of 300 is numbered and signed by the individual slimer.
#P47297 **$28** *each*

COWFLOPS

Hardly—they're a hit! Urban visitors to the country marvel at the soft, brown, pie-shaped objects that seem to grow freely in fields alongside rural roads. Little do they know that these bovine end-products can be theirs back in the city, too! Varnished for attractiveness and durability, our 100 percent organic meadow muffins make wonderful gifts as doorstops, paperweights, or table centerpieces. Shipped fresh.

Basic Cowflop #C11155 **$16**
Cowflop with Mushrooms #C11156 **$56**
Herd Collection (set of 12) #C11157 **$150**

EMU GUANO

There is no finer fertilizer on the planet than guano, and no creature on earth makes finer guano than a healthy adult emu. We keep a gaggle of some 125 of them at our company compound to provide customers with plenty of this marvelous stuff. We also offer a breeding pair that will walk about your property, leaving from two to three pounds a day of nature's bounty. Emus also are amusing to watch and fun to listen to as they speak emu to one another.

Aged Emu Guano #G15643 (Kilo) **$233**
Adult Breeding & Guano-Producing Pair #G15644 **$3,800**

Smyth & Hawk'em guanosseur Michael Czyczkrapski in the guano blending shed.

VINEBALLS

Weaving dead vines into spheres of ever-increasing size once rivaled collecting orchids and cross-dressing as national pastimes among the British ruling class. One of the most passionate of English vineball collectors was Earl Mount-Nanny, heir to a vast prosthetic penis and testicle fortune. In 1913, a single vineball Mount-Nanny had begun as a boy rolled off his estate, flattening a gardening staff of 30 on an adjoining property before coming to rest in the village of Marmalade-on-Crumpet, 22 miles away. Once again hot collectibles in the 90s, vineballs make a statement of one kind or another when placed on a lawn or in a home.

6-inch diameter Vineball #V89329 **$15**

12-foot diameter Vineball (shown here) #V89330 **$225**

The Mount-Nanny Vineball (120 feet high by two acres across) #B89331 **$17,950**

ENGLISH GARDENING STAFF DISCIPLINE PADDLE

The English have a long tradition of spanking one another when things go wrong, and, historically, servants and gardeners have been foremost on the receiving end. Now American property owners are beginning to discover the wisdom of dispensing discipline to their gardeners and landscapers on a regular basis. Our gardeners' paddle, crafted from solid English oak, is manufactured by Twickham & Haversham, purveyors to the Queen and the same company that has been turning out high-end disciplinary products for elite educational institutions such as Harrow and The Singapore Military Nursery School for more than two centuries. *Three feet long by 4 inches wide by 3 inches thick*

#S38022 $60

MOSSBALLS

Moss grows freely on rocks, well-shaded lawns, and in the vegetable bins of many refrigerators. When harvested in sufficient quantity, it lends itself to being molded into intriguing balls. Mossballs are like vineballs, only different.

Eight inches diameter #B99331 $18

DINGLEBURRS

We don't know what these things are or what they're really called, but they're all over the ground outside our office, they stick to our socks and our dogs' feet, and we've got to get rid of them! Dingleburrs' spherical design, ultralightweight and natural, Velcro-like adhesiveness must make them ideal for something.

Single Dingleburr #D40420 $1
Burlap Sack of 50 Dingleburrs (shown here) #D40421 $40

CLASSIC GREEK BIRD DINER

"Cheeseburger, cheeseburger!" That's what birds chirp when they fly into our authentic Greek birdfeeder, modeled after classical architecture and the Athena Diner in Southport, Connecticut. While the open-air design permits easy access, the grease-laden feeder food restricts flying for hours of bird-watching enjoyment.

Basic Hellenic Birdfeeder #B60710 **$135**
Feeder with Booths, Jukeboxes, Counter & Grandparents
 #B60710A **$175**
One Dozen Dried Bird-Burgers (ketchup extra) #B60711 **$36**
Bird Worry-Beads #B60712 **$12**

THE SMYTH & HAWK'EM BASIC BARN

If you want others to consider you a serious gardener, you must have a barn. Our basic barn comes preassembled on a flatbed truck and dropped anywhere on your property. Available in a "goes-with-anything" range of colors and choice of operative or purely decorative doors.

#B83277 *Basic Barn* **$5,875**
#B83278 *Basic Barn with nonopening doors* **$5,675**

GARDEN SAINTS

In troublesome times, we find ourselves receiving a lot of requests for well-made garden saint statuary. Until recently, however, we had to turn away many of the faithful. Then we discovered the superb masonry work of Dan Corleone of Brooklyn, New York. Dan proudly produces one model only, which he usually sells in pairs. "So's they got backup, you know what I'm sayin'?" His d'Assisi brothers are reputed to insure peace and harmony in the garden.

#S23617 *Pair of Garden Saints* **$354**
#S23618 *Triplets (for larger gardens):*
 Francis, Deano and Sammy **$420**

OUR SMALL CARDBOARD BOX

When we were kids, our grandmother used to have these tiny little cardboard boxes she kept tiny little things in. Now that we're big, most of our possessions are, too. But we noticed that we still had a few tiny things for which no appropriate storage system existed. We commissioned prisoners at Texas State Penitentiary to fashion these handmade Small Cardboard Boxes for our customers. They're great for anything less than medium-size objects and make the perfect piggy box for up to 28 cents in coins.
#B87356 **$3.85**

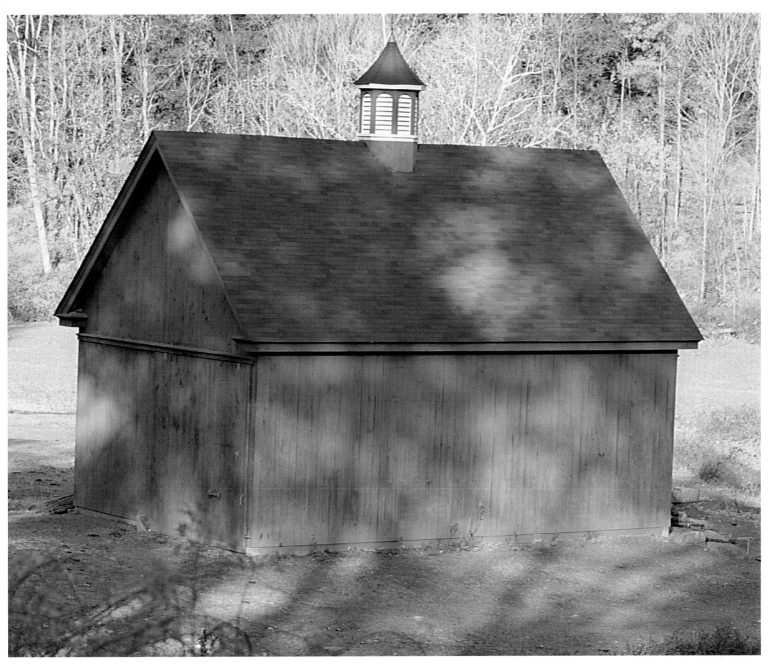

Vermillion Pavilion Red   *Lion's Mane Ochre*   *Lazy, Hazy, Daisy Yellow*   *Key Lime Green*

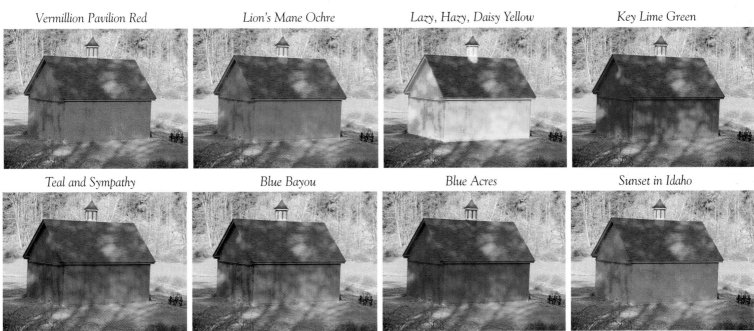

Teal and Sympathy   *Blue Bayou*   *Blue Acres*   *Sunset in Idaho*

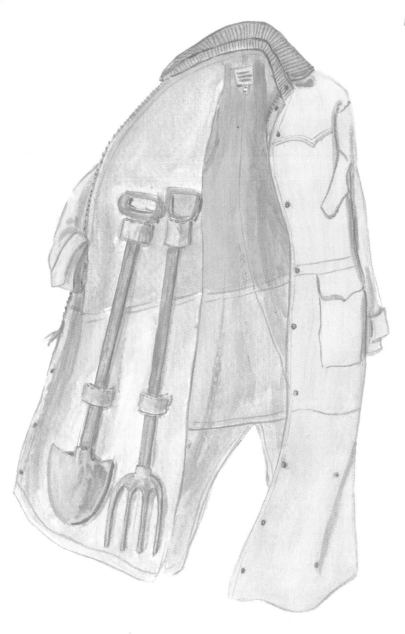

J. PECKERWOOD CLASSIC DIRTSTER

Dirty out. Somewhere in San Antonio. Or maybe Newark. Whatever. Somewhere. I'm feeling the way I used to as a boy. Strange. But talkative. I say things that other people seem to keep quiet about. I'd rather say than not say. And I wear things that other people don't wear. I'd rather wear than not wear.

Once, when I was seven, my father came home from the office to find me trying on my sisters' clothes. "What the hell are you doing, boy?" the great man demanded, his walrus mustache twitching and his mountain lake blue eyes glinting with either amusement or rage, I was never sure which. "I couldn't find any of my own clothes, sir," I stammered, though I was in my bedroom. "Also," I added, gaining confidence, "I thought I could improve on this basic design by letting the hem down a little and, oh I don't know, maybe throwing some canvas on the collar and a holster here or there." Father never entered my room again.

Later, in my thirties, I fell down outside Hussong's Cantina in Enseñada one night, fell right on my ass, got my coat all dirty. Actually, it wasn't my coat. Picking myself up and surveying the damage, I noticed I'd taken the wrong coat, one clearly belonging to someone a half-dozen sizes larger than me. (Confession: Glad the coat reached down to my ankles. Wasn't wearing any pants. Maybe never put them on that morning.)

"Hey," I said to no one in particular as I began dusting myself off, "this thing is really long. And really dirty!" Soon a crowd gathered in the street, drawn by my larger-than-life sense of style. It occurred to me that what people want are clothes that look as if they belong to someone else, to an actual person but minus the actual reality. I stopped dusting.

Today, this wonderful little gardening coat has become a classic. Simple, functional, elegant in its own way and, yes, still really dirty. Hell, I've found endive growing in the armpits of some customers' dirtsters I've inspected! Inside, the flap pockets and loops are roomy enough to hold everything from shovels and pitchforks to tractor tires and spare rocket parts. When not being worn, the dirtster readily converts to a combination garden shed and Port-O-San.

Although I don't garden (never have; vegetables, right?), I wear this coat for other reasons. I'm glad you asked.

It was while I was in Paris in the late 40s, driving a Duesenberg the wrong way down rue de Camus with a visibly anxious Hemingway in the passenger seat. Anyway, I was dodging oncoming traffic and thinking about my need for attention when…(*to be continued in the next catalog*)

Men's styles: Vain, Arrogant, Vainglorious, Insolent, Pretentious, Ostentatious. Comes in Plain Dirty, Dirty, Very Dirty, Filthy and Very Filthy #W34980 $198

John Peckerwood, an old friend in the mail-order clothing & accessories business, recently called from Katmandu with a pressing problem. It seems that the copy for his company's Spring catalog was running to more than a thousand pages of text, twice the length of the Vatican Gift Retail Shop catalog. Could he possibly borrow a page or two of space in *our* Spring catalog? Willing to do almost anything to get off the phone with him, we readily agreed. The following are several of the overflow items from the new J. Peckerwood Company catalog.

Collection

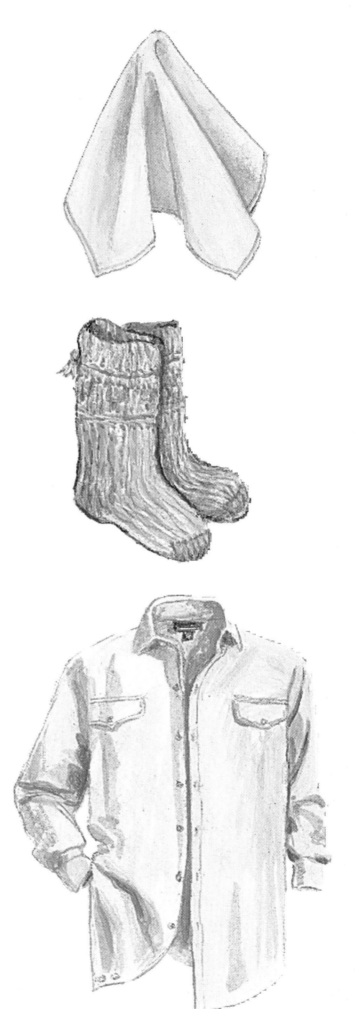

THE J. PECKERWOOD GARDEN HANDKERCHIEF

I learned everything I know about gardening handkerchiefs from the Maharaja of Jodhpur, Jr., during a fabric search I conducted in India in 1978. "You must never let them see you sweat," he would say. "Always use handkerchiefs of the finest pressed, starched Pima cotton with hand-rolled and stitched edges and you will feel confident all the live long day." "Do you love your garden as much as you love yourself?" I asked, hoping for a subtle insight into this complicated man. "You are a wise man to ask such a question," replied Jr. "I will answer you with a riddle: When a man loves the Earth, will the Moon be jealous?" He left me standing there, mopping my brow with a truly magnificent handkerchief.
In White Only. Garden Handkerchief #W04895 **$31.50**

THE J. PECKERWOOD TIBETAN GARDENING STOCKINGS

Some men can emerge from a mud hut looking for all the world like Cary Grant on his way to pick up Grace Kelly. Are they born that way? Some, like me, actually are. Others are lucky enough to be wearing my Tibetan Lounging/Gardening Stockings. A good pair of these stockings confers upon a man the propriety of a pair of silk stockings from the Lyon area of France, as well as the unstuffiness of a pair of wool socks from a fine Army/Navy emporium. Why these stockings? Because these are the stockings of Genghis Kahn, the Dalai Lama, and Bob Vila. Hand knit by Tibetan women over the age of 80 from the finest Ibex wool, the fine tailoring and hardy weave makes these stockings at home whether at home or at a state gardening occasion.
Tibetan Gardening Stockings one size fits men's 5–18 after soaking in water #W32493 **$22.60**

THE J. PECKERWOOD GARDENING SHIRT

In my wildest dreams I can't imagine venturing into my garden wearing a shirt unsuitable for the task at hand. Would you wear a polo shirt if you were about to operate on someone's brain? I think not. Would you wear a rodeo shirt if you were making a cameo appearance as King Arthur at a Renaissance faire? Ha! I've put every single shred of knowledge I've accumulated about gardening into this meticulously purpose-built garment. You can walk across your yard in full view of any mortal and hold your head up high because this, my friend, is a gardening shirt.

   Shoulders are expertly stitched to sleeves that end in cuffs. Buttons slide smoothly into precisely corresponding buttonholes. The collar is right on the top of the shirt, where it belongs, and the whole thing just drapes beautifully, held down by nothing but gravity. Isn't that the way it's supposed to be?
The J.Peckerwood Gardening Shirt
Men's Sizes 6, 6.25, 6.50, 6.75, 7, 7.25, 7.50, 7.75, 8, 8.25, 8.50, 8.75, 9, 9.25, 9.50, 9.75, 10, 10.25, 10.50, 10.75, 11, 11.25, 11.50, 11.75, 12 #W92834 **$156**

PRESTAINED CHINOS

If, like us, you've ever been caught in your pajamas on a sunny Saturday afternoon while your neighbors have been up gardening for hours, you'll appreciate our Prestained Chinos. Slip them on at the first knock on the door. You'll look as if you've been on your knees in the begonia bed since sunup! These beautifully tailored, 100 percent cotton trousers are stained with a compote of Georgia red clay, Kentucky blue grass clippings, and extra-virgin olive oil. The result is an exquisitely funky look that exclaims, "Whew, that was hard work!" *#K49080* **$80**

MUD BOOTS

Made in the country that invented mire, our genuine mud boots are constructed of peat uppers and a patented blend of high-quality muck and manure soles. Hand-daubed in Northern Ireland for an authentic look and feel, these wonderful boots slowly congeal around your feet and between your toes, to form a perfect fit. Also available in rain, slush, sleet, slog, and deep mierde. *#B20138* **$56**

MOW DE COLOGNE

Ten percent inspiration, ninety percent perspiration. That's the formula for our popular gardener's odorant. Distilled from lawn dew and migrant landscapers' work-shirts, a few sprays of Mow de Cologne will leave you feeling and smelling as if you've spent the entire day in the garden. Leaves a permanent yellow ring when dried.
Six-ounce spray bottle #C63812 **$35**

BURNT LEAVES

Remember the smell of leaves burning at the curb, filling the neighborhood air with the very essence of autumn? We don't—we're too young—but we've read that it was wonderfully evocative. Somewhere around the time we were born, state and federal environmental regulations banned the burning of leaves, and fall has never been quite the same—until now, that is! Our sugar maple leaves are gathered in New England in early October, then shipped to Mexico for burning. When a jar of Burnt Leaves is left opened in a room, the entire room smells remarkably like burnt leaves.
Six-ounce jar #B05407 **$10**

EARTH PUFF

Soil yourself! Just a few daubs of our powdery soft facial loam and you'll look and feel as if you've spent hours in the garden. More important, everyone else will think so, too! Comes in four shades: Topsoil, Subsoil, Mulch, and Manure.
#C26433 **$18**

FINGER-GARDEN RING

All the world will know you've got a green thumb when you wear this miniature garden on your finger. Our special growing medium of sphagnum and mucilage never falls out. Just plant the seeds you want and go about your business. Water daily in the shower and hang your arm out the car window to provide required sunlight.
#J62435 **$34**

FLOWER BASKET EARRINGS

A perfect companion to our Finger-Garden Ring, these lovely earrings are prefilled with an ultralight growing medium so they won't put an inordinate amount of stress on your ear lobes. They're also ideal for growing plants such as miniature hostas, which will thrive in the full shade of your head.
#J65265 **$12.65**

STRING-O-DINGS

Native Americans knew exactly what to do with the dried pod burrs that fell in profusion each fall. They sewed them to the edges of their tepee flaps to make highly embellished fringes. Later, settlers in Greenwich, Connecticut, attached the stems and pods to the tops of their shoes, thereby inventing the tasseled loafer. Since then, hybridization and a little genetic engineering have enabled these burrs to be snapped together to form endless strings for instant home and yard decoration.
#D60210 (*while supplies last*) **$18**

DE-VINE NECKLACE AND BRACELETS

When we introduced this charming set last season, we weren't prepared for the deluge of orders we received. That may be because this simple country look goes beautifully with everything from Calvin Klein to Osh-Kosh. Made from supple Scolioso Vines, these pieces are hypoallergenic and pest-free. When worn in the rain or shower, they sprout tiny buds and jewel-like flowers.
#V29877 **$98.65**

OUR FINEST GARDENING TROUSERS

Year after year, you've asked us to add more pockets to our most popular gardening apparel. Now these practically indestructible, 110 percent brushed-cotton, hand-battened, waxed and swathed, waterproofed, insect-proofed, mold- and mildew-retardant gardening pants have 42 individual pockets that will hold everything you people claim is indispensable. There is absolutely no more room for any more pockets! One size fits all. #T17180 **$54.50.**

"Growing a garden is the same as growing an empire. You buy the land, you hire the people, you fire the people, you rule the garden."

—Leona Helmsley

QUICK-DRAW HOLSTER

Peruvian-made Thinning Path clipping holsters were originally available only to members of the leftist landscaping movement that trimmed back much of Latin America during the 70s and early 80s. The spring-loaded release snap, high-speed swivel grommets and open-bottom holder makes this ideal for avid suburban gardening housewives, too.

Right holster #114760 **$79** *Left holster #114761* **$79** *Twin holsters #14762* **$145**

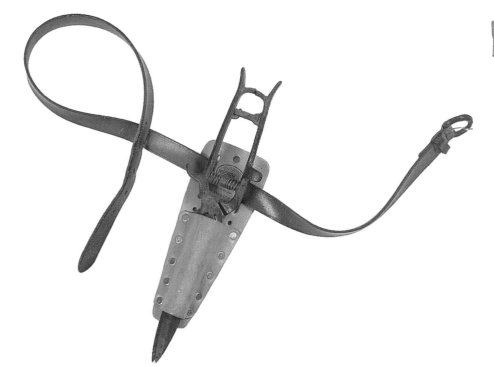

Loops for pruning shears, forcing snips, deadhead clips

Primary pocket

The Farmer's Almanac

Sandwich pocket

1,000-inch tape measure

Seed-packet pockets

Defoliant

Varmint poison

Credit cards

Prozac (or other prescription medicines)

Debit cards

Business cards

Cash for tips

Pocket computer with McGro software

Machete

Cellular phone

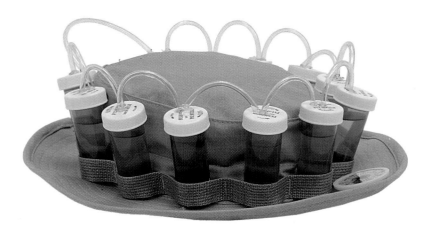

FARENHEAD SELF-COOLING GARDEN HAT

Why take a chance getting a hot head while deadheading? Knowing that cool heads prevail in the garden as well as the board-room, we developed this miraculous self-cooling hat that employs the warmth of the sun to superheat a patented liquid in special thermal transfer vials surrounding the brim of the hat. The convection that occurs quickly propels the liquid to 47 revolutions per minute around the Kevlar tubes, thus cooling and calming the wearer. Excellent on very hot days, during marital discord, before tax time, or as the best-ever cure for that occasional hangover.
#H12799 **$350**

DESERT GARDEN HAT

The timelessness of sand and cacti get updated in our fair-weather gardening chapeau. Now you can play golf, shop out-doors, or drive around town for hours with the top down and still maintain a beautiful garden. Note: The Desert Garden Hat must be worn in full sunlight for at least six hours a day; not suitable for climates that receive a half-inch or more of rain a year.
#H94001 **$55**

PARSLEY, SAGE, ROSEMARY & THYME TOQUE

Throw out those jars of dried herb flakes gathering dust on the shelf over the stove! Now you can enjoy fresh herbs grown year round not just in your own home, but on your own head! Developed for Chef Guy de l'Homme at the four-star l'Ennui in Paris, and previously unavailable to American consumers, our chef's four-herb toque allows you to pluck leaves from any of these four basic culinary herbs as you cook. Requires only that you walk or stand in direct sunlight a minimum of four hours a day.
#T14790 **$90**

SMELLINGTONS

No one has ever improved upon the classic Smellington garden boot. We find ourselves wearing our Smellies to our broker, our tailor, and any of the myriad other service people we must visit each day. As lovely as the basic black Smellies are, we saw a need for a larger palette to simplify wardrobe decisions. After working with the curator of New York's Metropolitan Museum of Art, we decided to mimic the color schemes of the Late Renaissance, with a little 60s' Pop Art thrown in for good measure. Now, you can wear Smellies for literally any occasion—cocktails, polo, the beach, the office, the gynecologist's, the cardiologist's, even your mother's!

#S22440 *Sizes 3–12, Every color.*
$150 *per pair*

Golf Pants Green

Double Espresso

Blue Blazer Blue

Envy Green

Imported Spring Water White

Beaujolais Nouveau

Cafe Latte

Lust Red

Lemon Torte

*Decaf Cappuccino
with Cinnamon*

The Laughing Moon-Beckstein Clinic

Born of pure Native American stock in North Dakota, Siouxie spent most of her childhood outdoors, where she was taught on the knee of her 123-year-old grandfather to love all living things. First at The Putney School, then at Bennington College, she studied botany, horticulture, animal husbandry, taxidermy, vegetal symbiosis, organic farming, scientific crop rotation, hydroponic gardening, holistic healing, alternative medicine, alternative psychotherapy, and alternative lifestyles. With her longtime companion Judy Beckstein, Siouxie has established The Laughing Moon-Beckstein Clinic for the Study of Near Death Experience in Plants. Her groundbreaking work with the clinic has earned her, among other honors, the Paxton Prize, The Pulitzer Prize, The Nobel Prize, The Bicentennial Swarthy Homestead Grant and the James Whitmore-Miracle Grow Endowment. In her spare time, Siouxie loves to make wreaths and flower panties.

SUMMER'S MORN AROMATIC PANTIES

Walk into a room wearing a pair of these exquisite organic underthings and hear people exclaim, "What's that wonderful smell?" That's your little secret. Summer's Morn is also the perfect panty in the kitchen when cooking seafood to counter fishy smells or in the summer when playing active sports. Comes in Rose, Lavender, Hay, and New-Mown Grass scents.
#P97864 Sizes petite to queen
   $9.95 *per pair*

DEAD FLOWERS

People love our dead flowers for their dry, lifeless look and low maintenance. We took perfectly healthy, expensive plants in full bloom, and we killed them. You won't find anything deader. Periodic dusting required.
One dozen dead roses #D00001 **$60**

"DEGRADES" FIFTYSOMETHING BIODEGRADABLE INCONTINENCE PADS

An entire generation is poised to discover the comfort and practicality, not to mention the necessity, of these wonderful gardener's incontinence pads. Made from absorbent lima bean fiber and the finest Eastern European burlap, Degrades allow boomers to garden far from a bathroom without fear of accident and embarrassment. Used pads can then be put to use balling seedlings or left to biodegrade in the garden or compost bin.
Box of a dozen #C04850 **$17.50**
Monogrammed support straps: add **$9**

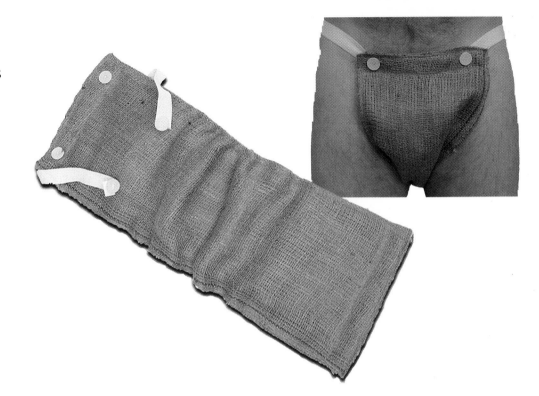

SHU-MIDITY 201S

If you've ever tried sampling the water content of your soil with a bad back, you know why we developed the Shu-Midity 201. Employing the latest space-age technology, these ultrasensitive and interesting-looking gardening shoes provide a continual status report on the humidity of your soil. Simply walk around the garden and look down at the built-in toe gauge. They're also handsome enough to wear to the club, where they'll tell you if the tennis court is dry enough to play on, and act as a lifesaver in the locker room, where they quickly let you know if there is any athlete's fungus afoot.
#S54235 Sizes 8–12 **$167**

OUR BEST DINGLEBURR SWEATER

We used to love the way our clothes looked after a day in the back acreage giving orders to the gardeners and landscaping crews. Often, we would come back inside to find our sweaters, in particular, covered with wonderful, natural patterns of burrs. After numerous inquiries from friends and customers, we hired a group of forlorn women in New Hebrides with nothing but time on their hands and had them sew the most perfectly shaped burrs on the finest Scottish knit sweaters available. The unique designs are reminiscent of those found on Druid ceremonial tunics. Yet because of the nature of the burrs and the idiosyncrasies of the knitters, no two Dingleburr sweaters look alike. These sweaters must be hung on hangers or laid flat when not being worn; once folded, they will remain that way. #S63268 **$456**

consumables

We expect a lot from our products, and our wreaths are no exception. It's not enough that they look attractive on a wall, door, or car grille; they should also serve a purpose. Nineties' homeowners frequently find that they've invited guests over for cocktails or dinner weeks earlier, but once the night arrives they're too tired or stressed-out to entertain. Our edible wreaths serve as silent hostesses and look good even as they're being nibbled to pieces by guests waiting in vain for someone to answer the door.

A. BATHROOM DOOR WREATH

Prunes are an increasingly popular fruit with the over-50 crowd. When clumped in sufficient numbers on metal frames and hung on bathroom doors, they achieve a collective colonic power that is felt throughout the house and is greatly appreciated by older family members. They also make for amusing little bathroom jokes when left on the toilet seat or bathroom floor. #W29613 **$50**

B. CHILDREN'S CRUDITÉ WREATH

What better way to get kids to eat their vegetables than to arrange them in an attractive manner and hang them on the door to their rooms! Sooner or later, out of sheer boredom or perversity, they're bound to nibble at the bait. And mothers love the electronic security system that unlocks bedroom doors only after the minimum daily requirement of veggies has been consumed. #W29614 **$55**

C. TARTARE HOLIDAY WREATH

Everyone swings into the holiday spirit when greeted with lumps of fresh steak tartare hanging on the front door. Our cold-weather tartare wreath with onions and capers lasts for weeks, given the right temperatures, and can be enjoyed by those living in growing zones -0 and 0 as late as Easter! #W29612 **$75**

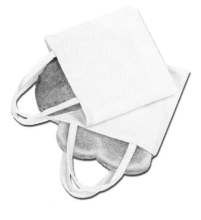

FORMAL GARDEN CAKE

Outdoor entertaining has just taken a seriously competitive turn. Now you can show off your garden and serve it, too! With a layer of ground dark chocolate as topsoil, our garden layer cake features sugar bushes and shrubs, iced perennials and climbing roses, glazed biscuit benches, and a marzipan birdbath. A second, rich vein of chocolate runs underneath the entire garden.

Standard Garden Cake #C36601 **$100**

Custom Garden Cake (send photograph or landscape architect's renderings)
  #C36002 **$200**

PUNKANUDOS

Premium cattails have become the smoke of choice among 90s' power-gardeners and celebrity environmentalists. Grown from Cuban seed in the wetlands of the Dominican Republic, and harvested by men in mustaches wearing green dentist's shirts, Punkanudos are rich, full-bodied cattails with frog and turtle overtones and a strong, swampy finish.

Cedar Box of 20 Punkanudos #C60512 **$189**
Silver Cattail Clipper #C60513 **$75**
Crystal Cattail Club Ashtray #C60514 **$95**
Burl Cattail Humidor #C60515 **$225**
Silk Punk Smoking Jacket #C60516 **$175**

INFUSED VINEGARS

Our tasty vinegars, made from 100-proof Russian white table wine and aromatic landscaping by-products, lend marinades and dressings a savory *je ne sais quoi*. They can also be drunk directly from the bottle. **Lawn Capers & Cuttings** captures the essence of wild animals crossing the property at night after a mowing. **Compost Zest** is redolent of potato peels, apple cores, rotting vegetables and virtually everything else you're likely to have thrown out during the past year. **Weeds & Twigs** contains weeds and twigs.

Lawn Capers & Cuttings Vinegar
#V71197 **$25**
Weeds & Twigs Vinegar #V71198 **$23**
Compost Zest Vinegar #V71199 **$27**

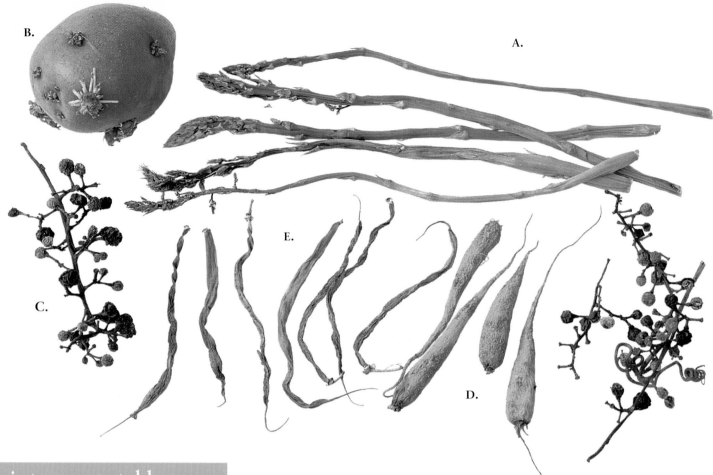

vintage vegetables

The history of vegetables is also the history of human civilization. The Greeks ate them, mostly spinach in salads and spanikopita. So did the Mayans, though usually as a garnish to the human main course. At any rate, the earliest vegetables to come down to us today are those that were hidden, thrown, or otherwise left uneaten. Our buyers scoured international tag sales, auctions, and private collections in order to offer this selection of rare and historic vegetables.

A. HOLOCENE EPOCH ASPARAGUS

We know little about this rare bunch of what is believed to be 12,000-year-old asparagi, other than that some young humanoid disliked them. The greens were found hidden under a grass placemat in a cave in what is now southern Florida, neatly laid flat to avoid detection until long after the primitive meal was over and the tribe moved on to another encampment. #V11574 **$955**

B. THE FINNEGAN

No one knows who threw this spud, but whoever it was had a great arm. What we do know is that a one-pound red potato hit Oliver Cromwell in the temple in 1650, knocking the haughty oppressor from his steed and marking the first glimmerings of Irish consciousness. The potato bounced off Cromwell and rolled into The Blarney Stone on Connell Street in Dublin, where, with historical foresight, owner Daniel Finnegan had it mounted and hung over the bar.
#V34555 **$425**

C. THE ROTHSCHILD RAISINS

From the extraordinary champagne grape harvest of 1809, Baron Gúy Mais-Oui de Rothschild spared only half a dozen bunches from the wine presses. His *raison?* Dry the grapes in the sun, then shoot them through a peashooter at the servants while they were carrying heavy trays. This *petite amusement* produced the world's first raisins, and the last of Guy's ammo has remained in the family vault in Paris until now.
#V71600 **$700**

D. PRE–WORLD WAR II CARROTS

Told that eating carrots would make her hair turn curly, Shelly Lefko, a 10-year-old from Brooklyn who liked her hair straight, stuck a serving of baby carrots up her nose on August 4, 1939, and was sent to her room. Two nights later, she did exactly the same thing and was permitted to stay. Students of early feminism have long known about The Lefko Collection, which we recently acquired from Lefko's children at an Otherby's auction.
#V43117 **$246**

E. FRENCH WAX BEANS

With lima beans and brussel sprouts, wax beans have repulsed children everywhere for centuries, including the young Napoleon. Happily for collectors, Mrs. Bonaparte kept everything her son ever touched or left untouched, including this rare example of early nineteenth-century wax beans. They were recently discovered, along with bad report cards, headless pets, a collection of training bras, and a size 3 general's uniform, in a family album.
#V98212 **$1,118**

LONG-STEMMED, CHOCOLATE-COVERED PODS OR BURRS

Nutty and crunchy, these natural treats (which look like dingleburrs but, you know, aren't, really) will surprise the indiscriminating chocolate lover. Eat them off the stem like chocolate-covered cherries or, better yet, leave them out for guests to sample.

#D20122 Box of two dozen **$24.50**

LOIN OF WOODCHUCK

He's gotten fat as a pig eating the cream of your crops. Now it's your turn. Despite a nasty temperament and an ornery disposition, woodchucks are surprisingly tender when baked, fried, fric-cassied, or roasted, as Chicago meatpacking executives have long known. Our chuck loins are aged for up to six months, then marinated in select herbs and 40-weight tractor oil. Order now for the holidays (sorry, only one order per customer).

#W45657 One-pound filet **$40**

OUR SMALL ROLLING PIN

Lots of great bakers work at Smyth & Hawk'em, and this has created a problem. With piles of cookies and cakes waddling in the door every day, we noticed that our gardening pants had begun to shrink. Abstinence proving considerably more difficult than we thought, however, someone had the bright idea to simply make all the baked goods smaller; that way, we could try everything but we'd be consuming less. We used pencils to roll out the dough until a friend showed us this superbly made miniature rolling pin from a very small town in Yugoslavia, ideal for making one 1/2-inch cookie. Bingo!

#B98749 **$12.65**

Exquisite hand-crafted tools are the foundation upon which we built our company. Take, for example, the line of imported Welsh "Pit Bull" gardening implements found beginning on page 52. We heard of a small smelting works in the Welsh town of Swarthing-on-Lumpstead that had gotten its start making precision killing swords for the War of the Roses but in the last century had shifted its focus to garden tools. That was all we needed to know. Like most of our products, these tools are inordinately heavy and excessively expensive. As they should be.

WETMAN PORTABLE DIVINING ROD

We spent thousands of hours drilling for water on our property without finding a drop. Then a good friend told us about the amazing Wetman. The first time we used it we got soaked! And now ours is the only catalog to offer this exquisitely crafted, portable divining rod "blessed" by legendary dowser Warren "Wetboy" Binksley of Dry Springs, New Mexico. Crafted from rare, native American hardwoods, chosen by Binksley himself for their hydrophilic qualities, the prethreaded sections are joined by the finest Royal Naval–quality brass fittings. When completely assembled and properly used, a powerful, water-seeking synergy is created. The Wetman comes with its own leather belt pack, and is always at the ready to tingle and dip in your hand at the faintest hint of water within a 17-mile range. *With leather carrying case and instructions.* #S23095 **$139**

SMITH & HAWK'EM LONG-NECK WATERING CAN

Some days are simply too hot to humid to leave the comfort of the air-conditioned house. But you know that if you don't get some water on those impatiens, they'll soon be toast. The solution? Just crack the window and water window boxes, door planters, walk borders, flower garden or the entire yard with our long-neck can. If it can't be reached with our can, you've probably planted it too far from the house.

#W87687 *6 feet* **$55**		#W87688 *12 feet* **$115**	
#W87689 *24 feet* **$245**		#W87690 *48 feet* **$510**	

ORNAMENTAL LEATHER TREE CLIMBING BELT

Nothing makes your lifestyle look more enviable than the presence of horse tack or tree climbing gear. We love to keep as many of these heavy leather items on display as possible. This musky, weatherbeaten tree climbing belt has the woodsy flair that will make the top of a coffee table in Manhattan look like it's in Lumberton, Oregon. And that's just the way we like it.

#T31214 **$128**

SET OF SIX USED GRASS CLIPPERS

Whether displayed as a complete set or broken up into individual show pieces, these wonderful, weathered, rusty grass clippers have the patina that usually comes after years of actual use. Just between us, they're brand-new. Leave them out and your garden shed will look as if it were the setting for an episode of *Victory Garden!*

#B58585 Set of six used grass clippers **$432**
#B58586 Weathered Box **$111**

OUR NO. 2 FIELD POTTY

As much as you love being outdoors, some functions are better left for the privacy of the great indoors. Yet no matter how carefully you plan your field trips, the time will come when you find yourself too far from a convenient commode and you will have no choice but to perform the unthinkable in the woods. That's when you'll be glad for the company of our unique product. Constructed of rubber-coated canvas, this indispensable tool hangs naturally from the shoulders in a way that permits you to achieve relief while remaining in a semiupright, unembarrassing position. The special "relief & release" strap in the rear gives you the option of dumping the contents in the woods or hauling them back to the compost heap with you.

One size fits all *#P76487* **$309**

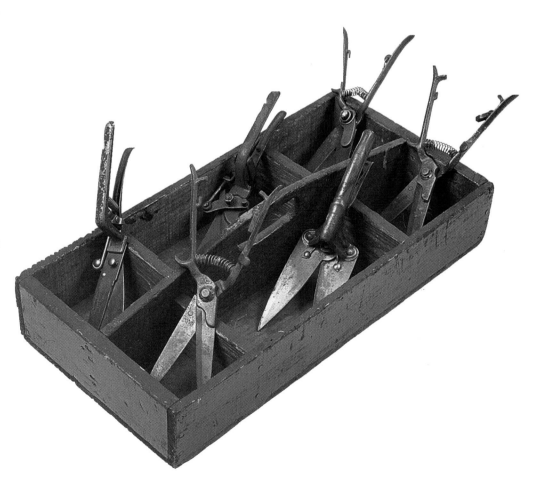

THE LANCELOT WOODCHUCK SPEAR

We could write a book based on the tips we've received over the years for getting rid of the common woodchuck. In our experience, however, nothing works better than grabbing this lethal little spear and jamming it into a burrow. While things can turn a bit nasty when scoring a direct hit, word quickly gets out to other woodchucks that your garden is about as safe as 42d Street and Broadway at two in the morning. #T74835 **$195**

OUR LARGE CHEESE SLICER

When you entertain as much as we do, anything that saves time is a real boon. This full-size, two-handed cheese slicer can render a 50-pound wheel of cheddar into bite-size h'ors d'oeuvres in less than 50 whacks. An added benefit is the high aerobic workout afforded by using our slicer on a regular basis. #T87678 **$80**

THE GUANO WHISK

The bats in our bat house produce an average of 125 pounds of guano a week, making for a superb fertilizer and a handy colorizing agent for our line of barn paints. But the common complaint heard from guano enthusiasts is that it tends to be lumpy. Enter the Guano Whisk. This wonderful tool whips the lumpiest doo into shape, creating a creamy guano with the consistency of soft, sweet butter. Your plants will ask you to spread it on them! #T76538 **$324**

Garden Tools

THE FALSTAFF VERMIN MACE

Ashamed that our hay barn was being overrun by field mice, marmosets, gophers, and every other species of four-footed menace, we developed the Vermin Mace with the help of our English arms expert and good friend, Teddy Dearth-Lafinghouse. According to Teddy's directions, sit on a stool in the center of your barn and stay absolutely still until you hear scurrying at close range. Then move through the barn making long, swinging motions with the mace, held parallel to the floor until every living creature is exterminated.

#T98748 **$721**

CHROMED BLUNT OBJECT

Sometimes, nothing does the job better around the garden or home than a blunt object. Whether for putting down horse, cow, dog, chicken, large fish, or an intruder, it's the most efficient and humane tool you can have at your disposal. This lovely chrome version has the added benefit of being lovely to look at.

#T48976 **$219**

THE MANURE ATOMIZER

This robust design has been in constant production since 1067, when it was used in the cleanup after the Battle of Hastings. To use, place ten pounds of two- to three-day-old manure balls on top of a solid tree stump. Then, wearing boots and a serviceable raincoat, stand off and take a good wallop. Within seconds the manure will atomize into a fine powder that is ideal for a myriad of garden chores.

#T42526 **$230**

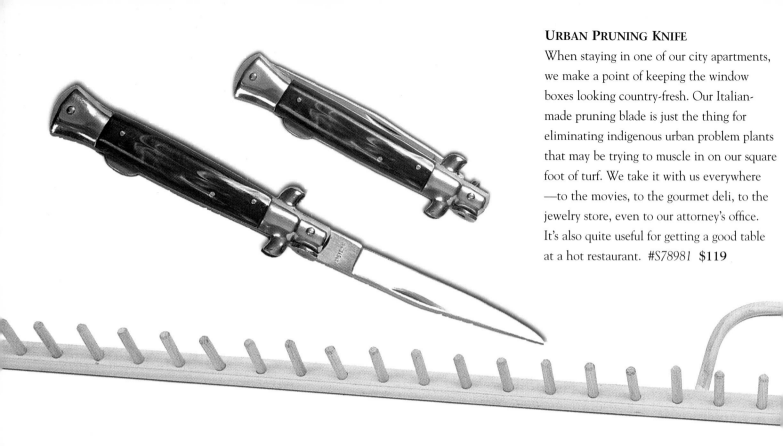

URBAN PRUNING KNIFE

When staying in one of our city apartments, we make a point of keeping the window boxes looking country-fresh. Our Italian-made pruning blade is just the thing for eliminating indigenous urban problem plants that may be trying to muscle in on our square foot of turf. We take it with us everywhere —to the movies, to the gourmet deli, to the jewelry store, even to our attorney's office. It's also quite useful for getting a good table at a hot restaurant. *#S78981* **$119**

ROBO-BULB SATELLITE-ORIENTED BULB PLANTER

"One giant step for gardening." That's what a friend of ours at NASA said when he saw our high-tech bulber. Simply load spring or fall bulbs in the cargo area of the Robo-Bulb, then set it down anywhere on your property. An onboard navigational computer calculates longitudinal and latitudinal coordinates from meteorological satellites and automatically plants bulbs in the optimum-growth sectors of the grounds. The perfect gift for boomers and others with back, knee, or other age-related conditions. (Advanced degree required.) Comes with textbook and long-life lithium batteries. *#R22701* **$2,248**

> *"I don't use* any *workers in my garden, all right?!!"*
>
> —Kathie Lee Gifford

SWATHMORE LOAM RAKE

We can never do enough gardening. But with our hectic publishing, marketing, retail, and mail-order schedules, there just doesn't seem to be a spare minute to spend in the dirt. The need for better garden-time management gave us the idea for this superwide-swath loam, grass, and leaf rake. Why waste time walking back and forth across the lawn or garden when you can rake the entire area with a single swipe? Now cover a full acre with just 96 strokes! The rake shown here is our standard 16-footer, but we will custom-make a Swathmore to any width up to 64 feet, at which point we run into shipping and ergonomic problems.

#S11980 16-foot Swathmore, **$189.50** *#S11981 36-foot,* **$249.50.**

For larger sizes, add $14.49 per running foot. Allow 6 to 52 weeks for delivery.

SWISS MARINES' KNIFE

Manly jobs call for a manly knife. The Swiss Marines, a seldom-deployed unit of Switzerland's national armed forces, use this big precision instrument for everything from nail and nose hair clippings to boat building and clearing paths over the Alps to the sea. Comes with spring-loaded belt clip and back brace. Includes machete, gorilla wrench, field guillotine, surgical limb hacksaw, bull neutering scissors, manual chainsaw, catapult, ATM machine, and jerobaum corkscrew.

#K11574 **$355**

furnishings

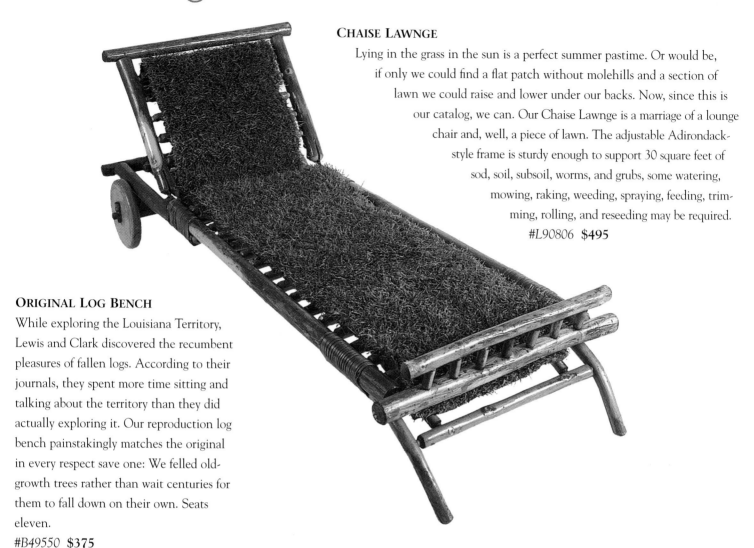

CHAISE LAWNGE

Lying in the grass in the sun is a perfect summer pastime. Or would be, if only we could find a flat patch without molehills and a section of lawn we could raise and lower under our backs. Now, since this is our catalog, we can. Our Chaise Lawnge is a marriage of a lounge chair and, well, a piece of lawn. The adjustable Adirondack-style frame is sturdy enough to support 30 square feet of sod, soil, subsoil, worms, and grubs, some watering, mowing, raking, weeding, spraying, feeding, trimming, rolling, and reseeding may be required.
#L90806 **$495**

ORIGINAL LOG BENCH

While exploring the Louisiana Territory, Lewis and Clark discovered the recumbent pleasures of fallen logs. According to their journals, they spent more time sitting and talking about the territory than they did actually exploring it. Our reproduction log bench painstakingly matches the original in every respect save one: We felled old-growth trees rather than wait centuries for them to fall down on their own. Seats eleven.
#B49550 **$375**

OUR DEEPLY DISTRESSED WICKER ROCKER

Nothing beautifies a garden or barn more than the passage of time. The soil gets richer, the perennials get hardier, and, after a generation or two, barn and furniture wood acquire a patina of neglect that says, "I was bought with old money." To us, however, the idea of waiting a week for anything, never mind a generation, is nothing short of impossible. That's why we're introducing this Shropworth Piffy-style English Wicker Rocker. It has precisely the right "look" we desire. But since it's made out of acrylic polymer, it will stay frozen in this glorious state of disrepair forever. Best of all, it can be yours tomorrow. #C82763 **$357** (*for same-day delivery by courier anywhere in the world, add* **$1,800**)

LANDSCAPERS' MOWING PLANK

We love the rough, weathered look and pure utilitarianism of this staple of the landscaping life. Without it, laborers wouldn't be able to unload the big machines that mow our lawns. With it, our customers can panel a den, lay a country kitchen floor, build a potting shed, or blue-collar a corner of the property. Our Mowing Plank comes precracked and warped. Not responsible for splinters. #P39930 **$75** *each*

LA CHAISE GRANDE

Do you remember any of your childhood? Most people don't. Due to neglect, abuse, or hundreds of other neurosis-causing factors, none of our friends got their first clue until they were in their late teens. That's why we love this "big chair" so much. Climb onto the seat and open up a treasure trove of "stuffed" memories. Within seconds you'll feel like a little kid again. Nearly everyone who has tried this wonderful time machine in our garden absolutely loves it. We must warn you, however, that occasionally the chair will open up a box or two in your psychic attic that might be better left sealed. If you begin to feel anxious, simply climb down and have a cocktail. #C54264 **$2,656**
(*Warning: This chair is not recommended for those in psychotherapy or on antidepressant or antianxiety medications.*)

FARM SIGNAGE

Primitive roadside signs once led customers to small farmer's gardens all across America, but not anymore. We bought up all the old signs! Now these charming pieces of folk art will tell your neighbors that you or your gardeners are capable of growing corn and other real produce in your garden.
#S35550 **$125**

AUTO WREATH

Few things better signal the arrival of holidays in the suburbs than a Christmas wreath hurtling down the road at 70 miles an hour. Our festive auto wreaths attach easily to most car grilles and come in an assortment of popular logos (domestic autos not available). Specify make, model, year, color, town of registration, personal education, club memberships, and annual income.

Mercedes Wreath #W53601 **$85**
Saab Wreath #W53602 **$65**
BMW Wreath #W53603 **$75**
Volvo Wreath #W53604 **$45**
Range Rover Wreath #W53605 **$95**

BIRCH BARK & LICHEN LAMPSHADE

Nothing makes a house in Scarsdale or Westport look more like a wigwam straight out of *The Last of the Mohicans* than a birch bark lampshade. Ours is made by a tribe that is still without casino income, so it's made to last. Stitched with surplus wild horse intestine on a frame of old Buick upholstery wire, our birch shade is left under several tons of manure until it has acquired enough patches of desirable lichen.
#L29675 **$159** (*tax deductible*)

FAUX VINES

If you've just finished a new wing on the house and don't feel like waiting 80 years until it's naturally covered with vines, we've got just the thing for you. Our faux vines come in preglued, 12-foot-wide sheets. Just unroll and slap one up on any exterior wall. Overnight, your prefab Raised Ranch will look as if the Duke of Earl had lived there all his life. #V57894 **$25** *per running foot*

classics

CLASSIC PAPER BAG

We've gotten so many letters from customers all over the globe asking us to bring back our popular Classic Paper Bag, that we have, but with a few late-90s improvements. Our new old bag is manufactured from second-growth pine pulp that's been dumped by a major lumber company, so it's earth-friendly. And the glue used in the bag is made from pork by-products, so the bag is animal-friendly, too. As a result, it isn't strong enough to be used to carry anything, but that's what makes it so classic!
#B54578 **$10**

CLASSIC STICK

There are times when the only thing that gets the job done is a plain, old stick. We use ours to move guinea hens around the yard, give directions from the side of the road, poke around under things to see if there are other things under them, and, best of all, make that neat whistling sound when we whip it back and forth through the air.

#S26266 24 inches long **$12.59**
#S26267 36 inches long **$14.50**
#S26268 42 inches long **$22.50**

CLASSIC CARDBOARD BOX

When we found our garage looking like a beer warehouse, we decided that we needed some good, old-fashioned cardboard boxes without a lot of shamelessly commercial logos all over the sides and top. Hence, our exquisitely simple Classic Cardboard Box. Made with particular attention to aligning all the angles at exactly 90 degrees, this humble beauty will hold literally anything that will fit inside it. Makes a great wall when stacked with several hundred of its brethren.
#B52678 **$20**

CLASSIC WIRE BASKET

You carried your books in it when you rode your bike home from school. Your clothes got stuffed in it when you swam at the Y. You tossed balls into it long before you got your first hoop and net. You're really old. That's why you'll wax nostalgic for our Classic Wire Basket, made for us in the suburbs by illegally detained Chinese immigrants from hurricane fencing.
#C77221 **$40**

BARN HAY BED

You'll wake up dreaming of barnyard animals after a night's roll in our hay bed. Posture-pedic and aroma-therapeutic, both mattress and frame are constructed of hand-baled alfalfa, timothy, and clover. Some assembly required.

King-Sized Hay Bed #H14330 **$235**
Queen-Sized Hay Bed #H14331 **$255**
Cow-Sized Hay Bed #H14332 **$285**
Hay Wall (12 feet wide by 8 feet high)
#H14333 **$195**
Field Mouse Starter Kit #H14334 **$35**
Barn Cat #H14335 **$45**

HAY BALE

Hay is a wonderful, natural medium with numerous practical applications: as a protective layer for newly sown lawns, mulch for sensitive plants and seedlings, and runoff barriers for new home construction sites. But, increasingly, hay is finding its highest use inside the home, where it makes for excellent night tables, love seats, beds, and, when clamped together, modular room dividers, wall units, even entire rooms.

#H11122 **$45** *per bale*

HAY CLOTHING FORK

While we love the idea of gardening, in practice it tends to get us a little dirtier than we'd like. Our Clothing Fork solves the problem. First, it keeps mud and dirt and stuff out of the closet. Second, and more important, it keeps our garden wear on display for our guests to see and envy. The Clothing Fork can also be ordered preloaded with soiled garden clothes for those who prefer not getting even the slightest bit dirty.

Basic Hay Clothing Fork #F54562 **$110**
Loaded with prestained clothing #F54563 **$510**

BARN BED BLANKET

What does this or any of the other items on this page have to do with gardening? We have no idea. But we do have a number of these blankets in stock, and they happened to be on hand when we were shooting this catalog. As long as you've bought the idea of the other nonessential items in here, you might as well buy one or more of these.

#B52965 **$160**

acknowledgments

First and foremost, thanks to Lisa and Jack Connor, Linda Downey and Jacey Haskell, Tom and Gertrude Connor, Betty and Richard Dorso, George and Del Grenadier, Mary Jo and Bill Cornell, Kate Coleman, Carol O'Rourke, Emily Gordon, and Joan and John Dunn.

Also our thanks to Suzi Desmond, Darryl Manning, Liz Hartstein, Myles MacVane, Ernane Campos, Kim and Margaret Rumford, Ellen and Tom McFaul, Kate Smith, Dale Allen Corrigan, Libby Hibbs, Bruce and Lisa Corrigan, Mike "Mow" Crechetta, Stephanie O'Rourke, Markley and Tucker Rizzi, Doug Ticotte, Maureen Kindilien, Maribeth, Skip Rastas, Roger Huyssen, Lynn Ogilvie, and Peter Pastorelli.

In Southport, many thanks to Jim Bleuer and Julie Bleuer at Casa Verde Gardens; Glenn, Nancy and Kelly at Village Hardware; Jack and Gerry Ringle at Switzer's Pharmacy; Ron and Shirley at The Jelliff Corporation; Chris Salko at Salko Farms; John Savarino at Indulgence Patisserie; and Leslie Model at Gordon LaReau. In Westport, thanks to Kevin Brawley at Tavern on Main; Jossan at Flower Fall; and Carl at The Flower Farm. And to Paula Lomer of Focal Point antiques in New Milford.

Special thanks and gratitude to Barry and Randy O'Rourke, Laura Campbell, Dennis Hayes, and to Mauro DiPreta, Susan Weinberg, and Brian Bondarchuk at HarperCollins. As always, thanks to Joel Fishman of The Bedford Book Works, Inc.